Tastefully Small

Dessert Canapés

BITE-SIZE SWEETS FOR EASY ENTERTAINING

BY KIM HENDRICKSON

Published by Atlantic Publishing Group, Inc. • 1405 SW 6th Avenue • Ocala, Florida 34471 • 800-814-1132 • 352-622-1875–Fax
Web site: www.atlantic-pub.com • E-mail: sales@atlantic-pub.com • SAN Number: 268-1250 • Member American Library Association

ISBN-13: 978-1-60138-267-2

Library of Congress Cataloging-in-Publication Data

Hendrickson, Kim, 1954-
    Dessert canapés : bite-size sweets for easy entertaining / by Kim Hendrickson.
        p. cm. -- (Tastefully small)
    Includes bibliographical references and index.
    ISBN-13: 978-1-60138-267-2 (alk. paper)
    ISBN-10: 1-60138-267-7 (alk. paper)
    1. Desserts. 2. Appetizers. I. Title.

TX773.H383 2008
641.8'6--dc22
                            2008015656
                10 9 8 7 6 5 4 3 2 1

COVER: Linda Kosarin
PHOTOGRAPHY: Trisha Solyn
FOOD STYLING: Alan Muskat
ILLUSTRATIONS: Leslie Kruzicki
INTERIOR DESIGN: Meg Buchner

Printed in India.

To my mom, whose creativity was never fully realized.

menues parceles ensemble sunt beles

small packages considered together are beautiful

13th-century French expression

Pomegranate Caviar Canapés, page 56.

Preface

For as long as I can remember, I've always liked small things. If my sister mastered making quilts, I would be content with embroidering the edges. If my dad and I worked on a carpentry project, I would work on carving the details; And when it came to baking, I got in the habit of taking any cake, cookie, or confection and trying to find a way to make it small.

Maybe it's the Gemini in me that requires variety. I can never make up my mind, especially when presented with a dessert menu. My belly wants it all, my brain tells me it just isn't possible, and my will finds a way. You're holding it.

I bet I'm not alone. For those who can never make up their minds, those who don't want a "whole" dessert, just two or three good bites, and those who will take any excuse to cook for the first two groups, this book is for you. Let's share a little more sweetness together. It's a small world, after all.

Cheesecake Truffles, page 30.

Acknowledgements

Where do I begin? So many people have supported me in so many ways. I hope I have thanked them all; if not here, at least with dessert!

As every writer knows, having a good manuscript doesn't mean it gets published. First I'd like to thank Doug Brown at Atlantic Publishing for his support. Thanks also go out to Chris Lundgren and Rob Laub for their help.

Second, good content is one thing, but the package is what everyone remembers. And I have Meg Buchner to thank for a colorful, attractive layout. The gorgeous photos took creativity, more than one keen eye, and endless patience. Alan Muskat's ability to see everything in my house as a potential prop brought life to my desserts. And Tricia Solyn's camera mastery came through once again. Add Leslie Kruzicki's watercolors to the mix and the result takes my breath away. Thank you all.

Patty Logan, Diane Cossin, and Mary Ellen Legge worked endlessly to correct all my typos, again and again. Proofing is now a testament of true friendship! To Kat Lau and David Burke, who supported me in so many ways: by answering the most minute questions, encouraging me when I thought I just couldn't make it, and just being all-round good friends.

Lastly, to Alan Muskat for his tenacious commitment to excellence. From overall composition and marketing advice to photo layout, and editing details, his watchful eye made this book better than I ever anticipated and taught me the importance of patience and perseverance. I am ever grateful for his help and support.

Table of Contents

Preface

Introduction

Fruit-Based Canapés

Classic Dessert-Based Canapés

Cookie-Based Canapés

Pastry-Based Canapés

Cake-Based Canapés

Bread-Based Canapés

Containers

Introduction

The traditional canapé, meaning "sofa" or "couch," is a cracker or small piece of bread with toppings: basically a miniature open-faced sandwich or pizza. Nowadays, people call any hors d'oeuvre a canapé just to sound sophisticated. But whether bread-based or not, these fancy appetizers are almost always savory. Why not make sweet bites for dessert? Is any other part of the meal more about flavor and beauty than size?

Move over caviar: the couch isn't just for potatoes anymore. Because there's no better way to fill a tall order than with small desserts. The reason is simple: it's the little things we love most. Who gets adopted first: the cats or the kittens? The puppies or the dogs?

Fact is, we go for the cutest, and that goes for food too: the little ones get all the attention. But while pets need a lot of it, these dishes do not. They may look demanding, but most are hardly so. People will say, "that sure looks beautiful, but it must take forever to make." Truth is, they don't. And much of the work (or play, I would say) can be done ahead of time, leaving you free to enjoy your event yourself. What a concept!

I've been teaching cooking for over twenty years and testing some of these recipes for nearly that long in the process. I've had hundreds of students tell me what they like, don't like, and don't understand. These dishes, including variations for every recipe in the book, developed in those test kitchens, and I'm thankful for the feedback.

But don't just take it from me. Let your own creativity shine. I decided long ago that if you want something done bite-sized, you have to do it yourself. That's how Tastefully Small got started, and it's how I encourage you to think. What inspirations have others belittled? Let them be little! After all, the smallest stars are the brightest.

From left: Persimmon Pavolvas, page 34; Coeur a la Creme Strawberries, page 32; Pineapple Granita Cups, page 22.

Fruit-Based Canapés

Fruit is the primordial food and the quintessential dessert. Bright colors and captivating flavors with no need for cooking or fancier packaging. But how do you cast old standards in a new light? From the inside out. Let beautiful fruit hold luscious fillings, making the familiar spectacular once more.

- Melon Flowers
- Lemon Coconut Nests
- Mango Almond Lychees
- Puddled Pears
- Pineapple Granita Cups
- Tropical Berry Kabobs
- Stuffed Strawberries

Melon Flowers

There's something about the color of melons that makes me happy even before I taste them. Add this mint pesto flavor accent and I'm even happier afterwards.

Yield: 24 flowers

1 large cantaloupe

1 large honeydew melon

1 large jicama, cut into ¼-inch slices

1 cup mint leaves, rinsed, patted dry, and firmly packed

2 ½ tablespoons sweet white wine

2 teaspoons sugar

1 tablespoon crystallized ginger, minced

1 ¾-inch flower cutter

2 ½-inch flower cutter

½-inch round cutter

3-inch round cutter

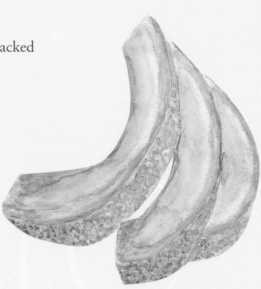

Cut melons into ½-inch parallel slices (no need to remove rind or seeds). From the cantaloupe slices, cut twenty-four 1¾-inch flowers and a ½-inch center out of each. From the honeydew slices, cut twenty-four 2½-inch flowers. Cut a 1¾-inch center out of each honeydew flower. Assemble two-tone flowers, then cut twenty-four 3-inch circles from the jicama slices.

Briefly pulse mint, wine, sugar, and ginger in a small food processor You want the mixture to have a fairly rough texture.

To assemble, place flowers atop jicama rounds and spoon a little mint pesto into the center (see photo, page 85).

Tips

If you don't have candied ginger, don't use fresh. It will be too strong. Add ½ teaspoon of powdered ginger instead.

Twists

Cut simple flowers out of pineapple with strawberries for centers and garnish with coconut flakes.

Lemon Coconut Nests

Lemon and coconut are a classic combination. One taste of a blueberry pie with a coconut topping, however, and the idea for this lovely trio was born (or should I say, "hatched").

Yield: 30 nests

4 tablespoons unsalted butter

¾ cup sugar

5 ounces light corn syrup

7 ounces unsweetened coconut flakes

¼ cup egg whites (about 2 to 3 large eggs)

Juice of 10 lemons (about 1 cup)

6 eggs, beaten

¾ cup butter, cut into small pieces

3 cups sugar

2 cups fresh blueberries, as garnish

Preheat oven to 375°F. In a medium, heavy saucepan, combine butter, sugar, and syrup and bring to a boil. Remove from heat and stir in coconut. Froth egg whites with a fork in a small bowl and add to saucepan stirring until well incorporated.

Place pan on medium heat and stir frequently for about 3 minutes. Cool.

Spoon mounded tablespoons 1-inch apart onto parchment-lined baking sheets. Press a well in the center of each mound with the spoon tip. At this point mounds should be about 2-inches across and ½-inch apart. Bake at 375°F until golden brown, about 10 minutes. Cool. Nests can be made up to a week in advance and stored in an airtight container.

To make the lemon curd, using a medium double boiler, combine the lemon peel, juice, 6 eggs, butter pieces, and sugar. Cook the mixture over medium heat until the sugar is dissolved, stirring occasionally. Continue to cook until thickened and just beginning to boil. Take the curd off the heat and gently lay a sheet of plastic wrap on the surface to prevent a skin from forming. Cool.

To assemble nests, spoon a small amount of lemon curd into each nest and top with fresh blueberries (see photo, page 85).

Tips

Shape nests with your fingers, making the base solid to hold the filling but leaving a ragged edge so it looks more like a nest.

Twists

Chocolate and coconut were made for each other. Spoon chocolate pudding into the center and garnish with chocolate chips, or nuts.

Mango Almond Lychees

Unless you have been served lychees in an Asian restaurant, you may have never had the opportunity to taste this heavenly fruit. The flavor is unique and refreshing. This special fruit dessert will expand your entertaining repertoire and leave your guests eager for more.

Yield: 40 lychees

8 ounces lychees in syrup, drained or
20 fresh lychees, if available

½ cup fresh mango, diced small

1 teaspoon mint, finely chopped

2 tablespoons almond paste, crumbled

Extra small mint leaves, as garnish

Drain lychees and pat dry. Slice in half from stem to tip, creating 2 open halves to fill. With fresh lychees, slice around and remove seed.

Combine mango and mint in a small bowl and carefully fill lychees. Lychees can be filled, covered, and refrigerated for up to 3 hours. Sprinkle almond paste on top and garnish with small mint leaves just before serving.

Tips

If lychees cannot be found in local Asian markets, ask your local Asian restaurant. Canned lychees taste almost as good as fresh, so keep a can on hand.

Twists

Chopped almonds and strawberries for filling make a great color contrast.

Puddled Pears

Pears are one of my favorite fruit and one not eaten nearly enough in the United States. This dessert has an intense pear flavor, and the spices and creaminess of the dairy add a dimension that just "sends me." Try them and you will see why.

Yield: 16 pear slices

4 cups water

¾ cup sugar

2 whole cloves

Pinch ground cloves

2 cinnamon sticks, each about 2-inches long

¼ teaspoon ground cinnamon

1½ teaspoons white peppercorns, lightly cracked

1 star anise pod, broken into pieces

4 large ripe firm pears, peeled, with stems left on

4 tablespoons unsalted butter

7 ounces crème fraîche

1 tablespoon fresh lemon juice

16 whole star anise, as garnish

Melon baller

In a large saucepan, combine the water, sugar, and spices and bring to a boil. Add pears and cover with a small pot lid to keep them submerged. Cook over medium heat until tender, about 15 minutes. Transfer pears to a plate to cool and reserve pot and liquid.

Pick any spices out of the pears and discard. Quarter pears lengthwise. Remove stems and cores (using a melon baller), leaving as much flesh as possible, then scoop a small well from the pear to hold the topping/filling. Cover and set aside or refrigerate for up to 24 hours.

Boil poaching liquid until reduced to about ½ cup, about 45 minutes. Strain syrup into a medium skillet and add butter. Cook over medium heat for about 5 minutes, stirring occasionally, until thickened. Stir in crème fraîche and lemon juice. Spoon sauce into pears. Garnish with star anise (see photo, page 85).

Sauce can be refrigerated up to 48 hours, but bring to room temperature before serving.

Tips

Crack peppercorns easily by placing them in a small plastic bag and hammering with a meat mallet.

Twists

Use green pears (Anjou, Comice) rather than brown-skinned ones. The green varieties are juicier and more squat, yielding more volume for filling.

Pineapple Granita Cups

The first time I made this granita I used it as a palate cleanser for a multi-course dinner. I never forgot its light refreshing flavor and decided to give it its own container for an easy and distinctive make-ahead dessert.

Yield: 24 cups

2 cups loosely packed fresh basil leaves

1 cup sugar

1 cup water

1½ cups pineapple juice

¼ cup fresh lemon juice

¼ teaspoon coarse salt

1 fresh pineapple, cored and peeled

Small basil sprigs, as garnish

Fill a medium bowl with ice water. Set aside. Fill a medium saucepan with water and bring to a boil. Add basil for 30 seconds or until bright green. Using a slotted spoon, remove basil and drop into ice water to cool. Drain basil and pat dry.

In a medium saucepan, bring sugar and 1 cup water to a boil over medium-high heat, stirring constantly until sugar dissolves. Add basil, reduce heat, and simmer for 5 minutes. Remove basil and let it cool completely.

Puree basil in a blender about 1 minute. Transfer to a large bowl and stir in pineapple juice. Cover and refrigerate for 10 to 12 hours. Strain basil mixture through a fine sieve into a non-metallic bowl. Stir in lemon juice and salt. Transfer to an 8-inch glass baking dish and place in freezer. Set timer and rake with a fork every 30 minutes until frozen, about 3 hours.

To make the cups, cut pineapple in half vertically and cut each half into thirds vertically to yield 6 long slices. Cut four 1¼-inch chunks from each slice. Each chunk should be about 1½-inches wide on the outside curve. Cut a thin slice off the inside curve so the chunk stands upright with the wide end on top. With a paring knife, carefully cut a ¾-inch well in the top.

Fill wells with granita and mound filling attractively, garnishing with basil sprig (see photo, page 12). Serve immediately.

Tips

For filling pineapple chunks, a large melon ball scoop works well.

Twists

Substitute pineapple juice with pear nectar and ½-cup fresh thyme leaves. No need to blanch, puree, or strain out thyme; just add to sugar water, cool, and stir into pear nectar.

Tropical Berry Kabobs

Angel food cake by itself seems to appeal to about half of the dessert eaters I've encountered. Bring fresh fruit into the picture, however, and the ratings double. This quick and lovely summer dessert will tempt young and old alike.

Yield: 24 sticks

One quarter of a 10-inch round angel food cake

24 fresh strawberries

1½ cups large, fresh raspberries

1 cup large, fresh blueberries

24 chunks cantaloupe or honeydew

24 red globe grapes

48 large mint leaves

48 large coconut flakes

3 Fuju persimmons, cut into 24 chunks

3 star fruit, cut into 24 slices

To assemble, skewer all ingredients in succession, contrasting colors, one per stick except for cake, mint and coconut (see photo, page 120). Top with star-fruit slice.

Tips

Place skewers in a vase or set into half a melon, flat side down, for a base.

Twists

Use lemon Bundt cake and fill hollowed strawberries with leftover lemon curd or whipped cream.

Stuffed Strawberries

The cheesecake filling in this recipe is creamy and fluffy yet quick and easy; the secret is starting with already cooked egg yolks. The result, like all versions of strawberries and cream, is irresistible.

Yield: 18 strawberries

18 large strawberries

4 ounces whipped cream cheese

2 hard boiled egg yolks, mashed into a paste

2 tablespoons sugar

Sliced or slivered almonds, toasted, as garnish

Melon baller

Pastry bag fitted with medium star tip

Slice off the top of each strawberry, exposing the interior, and cut a small slice off the bottom if necessary so it stands level. Using the melon baller, carefully scoop out the center.

Combine cream cheese, egg yolks, and sugar together in a small bowl. Using the pastry bag, pipe this mixture into each strawberry, mounding the filling decoratively. Garnish with almonds (see photo, page 85).

Stuffed strawberries can be prepared up to 12 hours in advance; keep them covered and chilled until ready to use.

Tips

Strawberries vary in size considerably, After trimming your berries, stand them up together on a flat surface. Trim bases further to make the group more uniform.

Twists

Leftover sponge or yellow cake can be used to create "strawberry shortcake bites." Crumble 1½ cups cake into a small bowl and add a few finely chopped strawberries. Spoon filling into hollowed out strawberries and top with a dollop of whipped cream.

Frozen Lemon Lime Bites, page 40.

Classic Dessert-Based Canapés

Tradition is a two-edged sword. There's a reason some desserts stand the test of time, but then there's sometimes good reason to change them. Many of our old favorites, while beautiful and delicious, can also be difficult to make and serve. Cut them down to size! These petite variations are prettier, more manageable, and a welcome departure from the same ole, same ole. Pay your tributes with a twist!

- Cheesecake Truffles
- Cœur à la Crème Strawberries
- Persimmon Pavlovas
- Tiramisu Napoleons
- Frozen Lemon Lime Bites
- Cranberry Poppin' Pies
- Minted White Mousse Cups

Cheesecake Truffles

Who doesn't love cheesecake? But sometimes a large slice, no matter how good, can be daunting. These cheesecake truffles deliver the same great New York cheesecake flavor in manageable portions. Forget petit fours; have five or six!

Yield: 60 truffles

2½ pounds (five 8-ounce packages) cream cheese,
room temperature

⅛ teaspoon salt

1½ cups sugar

⅓ cup sour cream

2 teaspoons lemon juice

1 teaspoon vanilla

6 large eggs and 2 egg yolks, room temperature

4 tablespoons butter

2 cups ground Zwieback biscuits (or graham cracker crumbs)

½ cup decorative sugar crystals

Preheat oven to 300°F. Mix cream cheese, salt, and sugar in a large mixing bowl until smooth. Add sour cream and beat at medium speed until combined. Keep scraping the sides of the bowl to make sure the mixture is evenly combined. Then add lemon juice and vanilla, beating until well incorporated.

With the mixer running, add eggs and yolks. Mix until batter is pale yellow and smooth. Pour into an ungreased 9 x 13-inch baking pan. Bake at 300°F unit mixture is set or internal temperature reaches 150°F, about 1 hour. The surface will be off-white to beige, not golden brown. Freeze for 2 to 3 hours.

While the cheesecake is chilling, melt butter in a small saucepan. Remove from heat and add crumbs, mixing until well-combined. Stir in sugar crystals and set aside.

Once cheesecake is firm, scoop out about ¼ cup at a time and roll into 1½-inch balls. This mixture is sticky, so you may need to dust your hands with flour periodically. Roll each ball in the butter/crumb mixture to coat the surface (see photo, page 6). Place in paper cups and serve.

Truffles can be frozen for up to 3 weeks and thawed at room temperature. The crumb coating will be a bit soft unless truffles are left uncoated until just before serving.

Tips

Work with no more than a quarter of the cheesecake at a time, keeping the rest frozen. This will make the rolling much easier.

Twists

Use chocolate ganache for a surprise center. Double the portion used for Yin Yang Cakes (page 82) and roll into ½-inch balls. Gently push chocolate balls into the center, encasing the chocolate with cheesecake. Roll each truffle in shaved, dark chocolate for added flavor.

Cœur à la Crème Strawberries

Cœur à la Crème is a classic French molded cheese dessert that is more cheese than fruit, but these little morsels balance the two. The perfect dessert for those who claim "most desserts are too sweet!"

Yield: 48 strawberries

2 ounces small curd cottage cheese

2 ounces whipped cream cheese, room temperature

Pinch salt

½ cup heavy cream

16 ounces (about 24) medium, whole strawberries, with green tops

½ cup strawberry jam, strained to remove seeds

Cheese cloth

Pastry bag fitted with ⅛-inch round tip

Small pastry bag fitted with ¹⁄₁₆-inch round tip

Press cottage cheese through a fine sieve into a small bowl. Add cream cheese and salt and beat until smooth. Beat cream into cheese mixture.

Line a small sieve with cheese cloth and spoon the mixture into the sieve. Rest the sieve over a bowl, cover with plastic wrap, and place in refrigerator for 8 hours to drain.

Cut each strawberry in half. Slice off the rounded edge of each half to yield 2 slices about ¼-inch thick. Spread slices out on a serving platter. Slices may also be stored on a tray in the refrigerator for up to 3 hours.

To assemble, fill pastry bag with cheese filling. Pipe out a heart shape in the center of each strawberry slice. Fill the smaller pastry bag with jam and pipe out a small dot in the center of the cream heart.

Tips

To ensure equal size slices and to save time, use an egg slicer to cut the strawberries.

Twists

Have no time? Jarred clotted cream is a rich substitute for the cream. Or fold seedless raspberry jam into some whipped cream and spoon on top of the strawberries.

Persimmon Pavlovas

The classic pavolva is a large meringue shell filled with whipped cream and fruit. Here's a mini version with a Southern twist: brown sugar, cream, and persimmon. Easy to prepare in advance and beautiful to serve.

Yield: 24 pavlovas

4 large egg whites, room temperature

¼ teaspoon cream of tartar

1 cup superfine sugar

4 teaspoons cornstarch

½ teaspoon vanilla

½ teaspoon distilled white vinegar

1½ cups heavy cream, chilled

¾ cup light brown sugar, firmly packed

3 Fuju persimmons, sliced into thin wedges

Mint, as garnish

Pastry bag fitted with ½-inch star tip

Line 2 baking sheets with either parchment paper or aluminum foil. Preheat oven to 400°F. Using an electric mixer with a wire whip attachment, beat egg whites and cream of tartar until frothy. Slowly add sugar. Continue beating until whites hold firm peaks, about 3 minutes. Turn mixer to low and sprinkle in cornstarch and blend well. Add vanilla and vinegar and combine.

Fill the star-tipped pastry bag with meringue. Pipe out 1½-inch rounds on baking sheets by starting in the center and spiraling outward. Pipe an additional loop on top of the outer edge to hold in the filling (see photo, page 12). Space meringues 1-inch apart.

Reduce oven temperature to 250°F and bake until meringues are dry but not browned, about 45 minutes. Turn the oven off and leave them in to continue drying out for 1 to 2 hours. Meringues can be placed in an airtight container and frozen for up to 3 weeks.

To make the filling, in a medium bowl using a hand mixer, beat the cream while slowly adding brown sugar until stiff peaks form. Fill the pastry bag with the cream and fill each meringue. Carefully place 3 slices of persimmon on top and garnish with mint leaves.

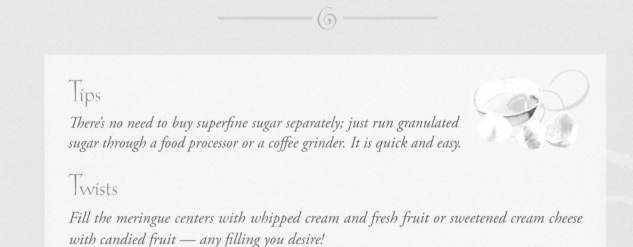

Tips

There's no need to buy superfine sugar separately; just run granulated sugar through a food processor or a coffee grinder. It is quick and easy.

Twists

Fill the meringue centers with whipped cream and fresh fruit or sweetened cream cheese with candied fruit — any filling you desire!

Tiramisu Napoleons

My friend Kat loves anything mocha-flavored so I spent a long time crafting her the perfect mocha dessert. Tiramisu has both coffee and chocolate, but what makes it so special is the cream. Napoleons, on the other hand, have that crunchy pastry (at least when they haven't been sitting in a display case). This recipe has the best of both.

Yield: 4 plated servings

¼ cup sugar

½ teaspoon cocoa powder

Eight 9 x 14-inch phyllo sheets, thawed

4 tablespoons unsalted butter, melted

8 ounces dark chocolate, chopped

1 cup heavy cream

2 tablespoons dry instant coffee

4 egg yolks

½ cup superfine sugar

½ cup Marsala wine

½ pound mascarpone cheese

¾ cup heavy cream, chilled

Confectioners sugar, as garnish

Cocoa powder, as garnish

Preheat oven to 375°F. Line 2 baking sheets with parchment paper. Combine sugar and cocoa powder in a small bowl. Set aside.

Unroll phyllo sheets and keep under plastic wrap to prevent from drying out. Place 1 sheet on baking sheet. Brush the surface with butter and sprinkle 2 tablespoons of the sugar-cocoa over the surface. Repeat with 2 more phyllo sheets. Place 1 more sheet on top and brush with butter. Bake until golden, about 12 minutes. Repeat process with remaining phyllo sheets. Let the phyllo stacks cool completely.

Prepare ganache by melting chocolate, cream and coffee in a small heavy saucepan over medium-high heat. Stir until smooth. Let stand until the mixture is the consistency of caramel, then spread half onto each phyllo stack. Set aside.

To make the cream, bring 1-inch of water to boil in a medium double boiler. Lower heat to simmer and add egg yolks, sugar, and wine. Cook, whisking constantly, until the mixture begins to thicken. When the mixture is thick enough to coat the back of a spoon, remove from heat and cool.

In a medium bowl using an electric mixer, whip the mascarpone until light and fluffy. Using a rubber spatula, fold the cooled egg mixture into the cheese. In another medium bowl, whip the cream until stiff. Carefully fold the whipped cream into the mascarpone mixture.

To assemble, using a heavy chopping knife, cut each phyllo stack into a 4 x 6 grid of 2-inch squares, 24 total per pan. If edges are ragged, use the knife to trim.

Take 1 square with a small offset spatula and spread 1 tablespoon cream onto it. Place another phyllo square, chocolate side up, on top. Add another tablespoon of cream and square but this time with the chocolate side down. Repeat with remaining squares to create sixteen 3-layered stacks. Using a sieve, dust tops first with confectioners sugar, then cocoa powder.

All ingredients, including phyllo squares, can be prepared a day in advance, but to ensure a crisp, light napoleon, stacks should be assembled no more than 1 hour before serving.

———————— ⟳ ————————

Tips

Keep pre-made phyllo squares in an airtight, cool, but not refrigerated container. Refrigeration is not necessary and makes it more likely, if the container is not perfectly sealed, that the pastry will lose its crunch.

Twists

Use lemon curd and whipped cream between the layers. Garnish with lemon rind and candied lemon slices.

Cranberry Poppin' Pies, page 42.

Frozen Lemon Lime Bites

The typical lemon bar never has enough zing for me. A little lime always seems to help. This frozen dessert is an easy make-ahead addition to any gathering.

Yield: 36 bites

1¼ cups flour

½ cup confectioners sugar

½ teaspoon salt

8 tablespoons (1 stick) butter, cut into pieces

4 large egg yolks

2 large eggs

½ cup sugar

Zest from 4 medium lemons

½ cup lemon juice (2 to 3 medium lemons)

½ teaspoon salt

3 tablespoons unsalted butter, cut into pieces

1 tablespoon heavy cream

Zest from 3 limes

4 large egg yolks

14 ounces sweetened condensed milk

½ cup strained lime juice

36 blackberries, as garnish

Mint leaves, as garnish

Line the bottom of a 8 x 10-inch baking pan with parchment paper, allowing the parchment to hang over the edges of the pan for easy removal. Spray paper with non-stick cooking spray.

Place flour, confectioners sugar, and salt in a food processor and process briefly. Add butter and process until mixture resembles coarse crumbs, about 10 seconds. Press firmly and evenly into the bottom of the prepared pan. Chill for 20 minutes.

Preheat oven to 350°F. Bake crust until golden brown, about 20 minutes. Cool.

For the lemon filling, in a medium bowl, whisk together yolks and whole eggs. Add sugar and whisk until just combined, about 5 seconds, then add lemon zest, juice, and salt, whisking briefly. Transfer to a medium saucepan; add butter pieces and cook over medium heat, stirring constantly with a wooden spoon. When curd thickens (about 5 to 7 minutes), remove from heat and stir in cream. Place a piece of plastic on the surface to prevent a skin from forming and cool.

In another medium bowl, whisk lime zest and yolks for about 2 minutes. Beat in condensed milk, then juice.

To assemble, spread lemon filling evenly over baked crust, then carefully spread lime mixture evenly over lemon layer (see photo, page 28). Cover pan with plastic wrap and freeze. Cut into squares or diamond shapes and garnish with berries and mint before serving.

Tips

Before adding the lime layer, refrigerate the lemon-layered crust uncovered for 10 minutes. This will make spreading the lime mixture easier.

Twists

Double the lime filling and omit the lemon filling. Just before freezing, drizzle a cup of strained raspberry jam over the surface. Then drag the tip of a knife or skewer through the jam about ½-inch deep in a spiral or waves to create a marbled effect. Then freeze.

Cranberry Poppin' Pies

Pies are one of my all time favorite desserts and this little version is a wonderful combination of tart and sweet. Better make two batches, or you'll be back in the kitchen by the time people taste them!

Yield: 24 pies

1¼ cups flour

½ cup sugar

½ cup packed light brown sugar, firmly packed

1 teaspoon finely grated lemon zest

½ teaspoon cinnamon

½ teaspoon salt

12 tablespoons (1½ sticks) unsalted butter, room temperature, plus extra for greasing the pan

2 large egg yolks

1 teaspoon vanilla

1 cup toasted walnuts, roughly chopped

1½ cups fresh cranberries

⅓ cup sugar

⅛ cup water

24-cup miniature muffin pan (⅛ cup size cups)

Preheat oven to 375°F. Pulse flour, sugar, brown sugar, lemon zest, cinnamon, and salt in a food processor until combined. Add butter and pulse until mixture resembles coarse meal. Add egg yolks and vanilla and process until the mixture comes together into dough.

Place 1 cup of dough into a small bowl and stir in walnuts. Set aside for topping.

Butter the bottom and sides of each muffin cup and evenly press 1 tablespoon of dough into each pan. Chill until dough is firm, about 20 minutes.

In a small saucepan, combine cranberries, sugar, and water. Cook over medium-high heat, stirring with a wooden spoon occasionally, until cranberries pop.

When cranberries have cooled, fill the muffin cups evenly. Crumble the reserved dough on top of each pie (see photo, page 39). Bake for 20 to 25 minutes until golden brown and filling is bubbling. Cool completely in the pan. Remove carefully using a sharp knife.

Poppin' Pies can be made ahead and stored in an airtight container for up to 10 days.

Tips

Cranberries too tart for you? Double the sugar to sweeten.

Twists

Strawberry, blueberry, and pineapple also work well. Simmer fruit until it softens and liquid becomes syrupy, about 5 to 7 minutes.

Minted White Mousse Cups

Many people say white chocolate is just not their cup of tea, yet this dessert seems to be loved by all. Originally one element of a more complicated layered recipe, I felt this mousse has enough character to stand on its own.

Yield: 12 cups

1 pound white chocolate, chopped

½ teaspoon unflavored gelatin

7 tablespoons heavy cream

¼ teaspoon mint extract

1⅓ cups heavy cream, chilled

6 ounces semi-sweet chocolate, chopped

½ cup heavy cream

12 small raspberries, as garnish

12 mint leaves, as garnish

12 demitasse cups or small china tea cups

Pastry bag fitted with ⅛-inch round tip

Melt white chocolate in a double boiler over barely simmering water, stirring until smooth. Remove pan from the heat and set aside.

In a small, heavy saucepan, sprinkle gelatin over 7 tablespoons cream. Let stand 10 minutes to soften. Cook over low heat until gelatin dissolves, stirring constantly. Whisk warmed cream into melted chocolate. Stir in mint extract. Transfer to a large bowl. Let stand until cool but not set, about 5 minutes.

Using an electric mixer, beat 1⅓ cups heavy cream to soft peaks. Fold half into white chocolate mixture to lighten, then gently fold in the rest. Spoon mousse equally into 12 cups.

To prepare the dark chocolate ganache, melt the chocolate and cream in a small, heavy saucepan over med-low heat, stirring until smooth. Cool until it is the consistency of molasses. Spoon ganache into pastry bag. Starting at the center of each cup, pipe a spiral over the surface. Place a raspberry and mint leaf in the center and chill until set.

Tips

When melting white chocolate, keep in mind that it gets soft and "gloppy" but never liquid like milk or dark chocolate, so be careful not to burn it.

Twists

Substitute orange flavoring for the mint extract, tint a cup of mousse with orange food coloring for the spiral and garnish with orange zest and a mint leaf.

Passion Fruit Oysters, page 50.

46

Cookie-Based Canapés

Who doesn't love cookies? This canapé collection gives the average cookie new life purpose. Teamed with delicious toppings, these crispy foundations add flair and ease of enjoyment. Now you just need a fancy glass for the milk or tea.

- Hazelnut Mousse Delights
- Passion Fruit Oysters
- Toffee-Nut Bites
- Choco-Ginger Sandwiches
- Pomegranate Caviar Canapés

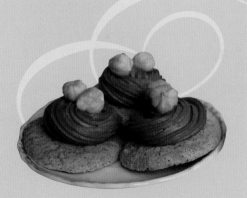

Hazelnut Mousse Delights

You know you have a winner when you can't stop tasting the batter. It's no wonder these are just as popular among friends today as the first time I served them, many years ago. Now this old standby gets an elegant facelift with a touch of chocolate mousse.

Yield: 32 cookies

2 cups hazelnuts, toasted, skins removed

¾ cup sugar, divided

5 large egg whites, room temperature

⅓ cup flour

5 tablespoons butter, melted and cooled

16 ounces bittersweet chocolate, chopped small

1 cup heavy cream, chilled

2 tablespoons dark rum or strong coffee

4 egg whites, room temperature

½ cup sugar

1 cup hazelnuts, toasted, skinned, and halved, as garnish

Pastry bag fitted with a ½-inch round tip

Preheat oven to 350°F. Toast nuts on a baking sheet, shaking pan occasionally, until fragrant, about 10 minutes. Nuts will burn soon after they start to smell toasted, so be careful. Lower temperature to 275°F. In a food processor, finely chop nuts with ¼ cup sugar and set aside.

In a large bowl, beat the egg whites at high speed, sprinkling the remaining sugar in slowly, 1 tablespoon at a time. Beat until sugar is dissolved and stiff peaks form. Using a rubber spatula, fold in hazelnuts and flour, then drizzle in butter and carefully but thoroughly fold to combine.

Pipe or drop the batter onto parchment-lined baking sheets in 1-inch rounds. Cookies will spread to 2-inches so space the batter 1½-inches apart. Bake 2 sheets at a time, rotating sheets when half done, until cookies are firm and edges are golden brown, about 25 minutes. Cool on pan. Cookies can be kept in an airtight container for 3 weeks.

To prepare the mousse, whisk chocolate and cream together in a heavy, medium saucepan over medium heat until chocolate melts. Stir in rum and cool. Pour egg whites and sugar into a small bowl and heat over a small pot with 1-inch of boiling water for 3 minutes. Take off the heat and cool for 1 minute. Using an electric mixer, whip egg whites to stiff peaks. Fold into the cooled chocolate mixture in three stages. Press a piece of plastic wrap on the surface to prevent a skin from forming and chill for 1 to 2 hours.

To assemble, fill pastry bag with mousse. Pipe a decorative mound of mousse on each cookie surface and garnish with half a hazelnut (see photo, page 65). If mousse is difficult to pipe or comes out ragged, it's probably too cold. Let it warm up a bit and try again.

Tips

If hazelnut skins do not blister off after toasting, rub them between 2 towels while still hot. If some bits remain, just use these nuts for the cookies; the speckles add a nice effect.

Twists

Hazelnut and coffee flavor pair well. Instead of chocolate mousse, whip 1½- cups heavy cream and fold in 1 cup finely chopped hazelnuts and 1 tablespoon espresso powder.

Passion Fruit Oysters

I don't know what part of this dessert I like better, the filling or the base. Floating atop rich butter wafers, the unforgettable flavor of passion fruit always earns its name. My mouth begins to water just thinking about it.

Yield: 36 oysters

12 tablespoons (1½ sticks) unsalted butter, room temperature

⅓ cup sugar

1 large egg

1 teaspoon vanilla

¾ cup flour

½ cup sugar

½ cup passion fruit puree

1 cup milk chocolate, chopped

1 cup white chocolate, chopped

2½ ounces heavy cream

8 tablespoons (1 stick) unsalted butter, room temperature, cut into 8 pieces

3½ ounce bar white chocolate (like Lindt)

Pastry bag fitted with ½-inch round tip

Pastry bag fitted with ¾-inch star tip

¼-inch round metal pastry tip

Preheat oven to 350°F. With a mixer, cream the butter and sugar on low speed until pale and fluffy. Add the egg and vanilla and continue to mix.

Gradually add flour and mix until well blended. Fill the round-tipped pastry bag with batter. Pipe ½-to ¾-inch rounds onto parchment-lined baking sheets, spaced 1-inch apart. Bake until edges are brown, about 10 minutes, and cool. Wafers can be stored in an airtight container for up to a week.

To prepare the ganache, in a small frying pan on medium heat, sprinkle in sugar. With a wooden spoon, gently stir until it starts to melt, watching carefully to make sure it doesn't burn. Once all of the sugar is melted and has turned a caramel color, carefully pour the passion fruit puree into the pan. The sugar will sputter, so be careful. It will then seize up and harden. Continue gently stirring until the mixture completely melts again. Set aside.

Place both chocolates into a medium bowl. In a small saucepan, bring cream to a boil, then pour over chocolate. Stir until smooth. Pour passion fruit caramel into the chocolate and stir until smooth. While mixture is still warm, add butter, one piece at a time, combining completely before adding the next. Let ganache set until it is the texture of peanut butter.

To make the pearls, use the ¼-inch pastry tip to cut rounds out of the white chocolate bar.

To assemble, fill the star-tipped pastry bag with ganache. Decoratively pipe out about 1 tablespoon of ganache onto a butter wafer, then press another wafer on top on an angle. Repeat for all wafers and place a pearl in each oyster (see photo, page 46).

Tips

Short on time? Use silver dragees for pearls.

Twists

Brown sugar cream, clotted cream, and Nutella all make delicious fillings. Spread half an inch of filling between two wafers like a sandwich. Dust with powdered sugar.

Toffee-Nut Bites

Exquisitely decadent, these chewy nut clusters riding on rich butter cookies are as easy as they are beautiful — but that's between us!

Yield: 24 open sandwiches

2 cups flour

¼ teaspoon baking powder

¼ teaspoon salt

1 cup butter, softened

½ cup confectioners sugar

4 tablespoons butter

½ cup brown sugar, firmly packed

4 tablespoons light corn syrup

1¼ cups lightly salted mixed nuts

1 teaspoon vanilla

Combine flour, baking powder, and salt in small bowl. In a large bowl, beat the butter and sugar together with a mixer on high speed for 5 minutes. The mixture should be light and fluffy. At low speed, add flour mixture and beat until just incorporated. Wrap dough in plastic wrap and refrigerate for 2 hours.

Preheat oven to 375°F. Line a 9 x 9-inch square pan with parchment paper, leaving some paper hanging over two opposite ends of the pan. This will make lifting the shortbread out easier.

Press dough evenly into pan. Using a fork, score dough into a 6 x 6-inch grid of thirty-six 1½-inch squares. Bake about 20 minutes or until edges are lightly colored. While dough is still warm, cut into squares along fork marks with a sharp knife. Let dough cool completely. Remove shortbread and gently cut apart the squares.

To make the topping, in a heavy saucepan, combine the butter, brown sugar, and corn syrup. Bring to a boil over medium heat. Remove from heat and stir in nuts and vanilla.
Cool for 15 minutes. Spoon warm nut mixture on top of each square.
Let them stand for 20 minutes while topping sets.

———————— ⟳ ————————

Tips

No stopping when topping. The toffee-nut mixture firms up quickly: by the time you get to the last few squares, it may be too thick to work with. If so, gently reheat the mixture over a double boiler until it is more pliable.

Twists

Reduce nuts to ¼ cup and add ½ cup chocolate chips and ½ cup flaked coconut. Yum!

Choco-Ginger Sandwiches

If you think ice cream sandwiches are for children, make this version — and see if it gets to them! The chocolate cookie alone is one of the best I've ever tasted. Paired with ginger ice cream, this is definitely one for the grown-ups.

Yield: 20 sandwiches

1 tablespoon freshly-grated ginger

8 tablespoons (1 stick) unsalted butter, room temperature

½ cup dark brown sugar, firmly packed

¼ cup unsulfured molasses

1½ cups flour

1 teaspoon baking soda

1¼ teaspoons ground ginger

1 teaspoon ground cloves

¼ teaspoon ground nutmeg

1 tablespoon cocoa powder

7 ounces semi-sweet chocolate, finely chopped

¼ cup granulated sugar, for rolling cookies

2 cups vanilla ice cream (good quality, high butterfat)

4 teaspoons grated ginger

1 cup semi-sweet chocolate, finely chopped, as garnish

Preheat oven to 325°F. Using an electric mixer, cream the tablespoon of grated ginger and butter until light and fluffy, about 4 minutes. Add the brown sugar, then the molasses, and beat until combined.

Mix flour, baking soda, ginger, cloves, nutmeg, and cocoa together in a small bowl. Gradually add to the butter/sugar until fully incorporated. Stir in the chocolate and chill dough until firm, about 30 minutes.

Shape dough into 1-inch balls. Place ¼ cup sugar in a pie pan and roll each ball in it. Place sugared balls on parchment-lined baking sheets, about 1-inch apart. Bake until surface cracks slightly, about 12 to 14 minutes. Cool.

Place ice cream in a medium bowl. Using a rubber spatula, soften and stir in the grated ginger. Freeze until firm.

To assemble, spread enough ice cream on one cookie to create a layer about ½-inch thick. Top with another cookie to create a sandwich. Roll the exposed ice cream edges in chopped chocolate (see photo, page 124). Sandwiches can be frozen until ready to use.

Tips

If the ice cream is difficult to scoop and spread, use an ice cream scoop and a small metal spatula, respectively, for each step.

Twists

Use butter wafers from Passion Fruit Oyster recipe (page 50) for even smaller ice cream sandwiches. Replace ginger ice cream with any good fruit-flavored ice cream, then roll edges in chopped almonds.

Pomegranate Caviar Canapés

Long before pomegranate became fashionable, it held special significance for me. My grandmother would buy one — just one, for they were expensive — each Christmas. We would all sit in the kitchen with dish towels around our necks while we savored the ruby-like fruit. I give you this more elegant presentation in her honor. You supply the bibs!

Yield: 20 canapés

3 medium pomegranates

16 tablespoons (2 sticks) unsalted butter, room temperature

⅓ cup heavy cream

2 cups flour

Sugar

1 cup honey

¾ cup sharp cheddar cheese, finely grated, as garnish

3-inch round cutter

Score the rind of each pomegranate. Remove the seeds and place them in a bowl lined with a paper towel. 3 pomegranates should yield about three cups of seeds. Set aside.

Cream the butter, heavy cream, and flour in a medium bowl using a rubber spatula or hand mixer. Cover and chill dough for 1 hour or until firm. Pour some sugar in a shallow dish and set aside.

Preheat oven to 375°F. Take ⅓ of the dough from the refrigerator and roll out on a lightly floured surface to ⅛-inch thickness. Cut out 3-inch rounds from the dough. Press rounds firmly into the sugar to ensure that it sticks, and place on parchment-lined baking pans 1-inch apart. Prick each round with a fork a few times. Repeat with remaining dough to yield 20 rounds total. Bake 10 minutes or until the bottom and edges are lightly browned. Cool.

Combine pomegranate seeds and honey. Spoon 2 tablespoons pomegranate seeds onto the center of each round and top with a sprinkling of grated cheddar (see photo, page 59). Serve at once.

––––––––––––––––– ⟳ –––––––––––––––––

Tips

To separate pomegranates without the mess, do it underwater.

Twists

Raspberries and blackberries with honey make a flavorful alternative. Crumble almond biscotti on top as a garnish.

From left: Lady Apple Crisp, page 12; Rustic Strawberry Rhubarb Tarts, page 60; Toasted Banana Flowers, page 98.

Pastry-Based Canapés

Pastry is the gift wrap of the dessert world. Delicious fillings beckon, but too often we throw out the wrapping paper. Not with these novelties. Whether it's a traditional strawberry rhubarb tart or an unusual raspberry tangerine bundle, these consummate containers will hold their own. No more piles of plates with the crust left behind!

- Rustic Strawberry Rhubarb Tarts
- Grapefruit Orange Canapés
- Raspberry-Tangerine Bundles
- Lime Cream Squares
- Caramelized Banana Canapés
- Twelve Layer Bites

Rustic Strawberry Rhubarb Tarts

Anything with rhubarb in it reminds me once again of my grandmother, out in the garden, breaking off stalks destined for a cloying end. Even sugar by the cupful, however, couldn't match the tartness or mask the texture of stewed rhubarb. Only my father and I – and grandmother, of course – enjoyed it.

This classic combination of strawberry and rhubarb, together in a buttery cheese pastry, is the choice of a new generation. I challenge you to eat just one!

Yield: 30 tarts

2⅔ cups cake flour, sifted

½ teaspoon salt

¼ teaspoon baking powder

8 ounces cream cheese, softened

16 tablespoons (2 sticks) unsalted butter, room temperature

2 tablespoons confectioners sugar

2 large egg yolks

1 tablespoon sour cream

1 tablespoon vanilla

2 tablespoons unsalted butter

1 cup fresh or frozen rhubarb, cut into small dice

1 cup fresh strawberries, cut into small dice

¼ cup sugar

3-inch round cutter

In a medium bowl, whisk the flour, salt, and baking powder together. In a separate bowl using an electric mixer, cream the cream cheese, butter, and sugar until smooth. Add egg yolks, sour cream, and vanilla and mix to incorporate. At low speed, add dry ingredients until just combined. Remove dough and divide in half, rolling each half into a disc. Wrap each disc in plastic wrap and chill for 1 to 6 hours.

In a small frying pan over medium heat, melt butter and sauté rhubarb, strawberries, and sugar until the liquid evaporates and the mixture is thickened, about 10 minutes. Cool.

Preheat oven to 325°F. Roll both chilled disks to ⅛-inch thickness and cut 15 rounds from each. Spoon a rounded teaspoon of strawberry filling onto the center of each round. Fold and pinch the dough edges up and around the filling, leaving the center exposed. The edges of the crust can be rough and rustic-looking (see photo, page 58).

Place filled tarts on a parchment-lined baking sheet spaced 1-inch apart. Bake for 20 minutes or until edges are lightly browned. Cool before serving.

Tips

Fresh rhubarb freezes well, so when you find it, stock up. Simply cut into chunks and freeze in an airtight container.

Twists

Bake empty tart crusts until lightly browned. Cool. Crumble a bit of marzipan on the bottom of each, then spoon a little raspberry or strawberry jam on top and sprinkle with almond slices.

Grapefruit Orange Canapés

Grapefruit, pastry cream, and cornmeal. Who would've thunk it? And yet, at the pie and tart class I taught for many years, this recipe was a consistent success. Mystify friends with this sure-fire surprise.

Yield: 16 canapés

1½ cups flour

¾ cup finely ground cornmeal

¾ teaspoon salt

12 tablespoons (1½ sticks) unsalted butter, room temperature

¾ cup sugar

2 large eggs

Egg wash (1 egg mixed with 2 tablespoons water)

1 cup whole milk

⅓ cup sugar

3 egg yolks

Pinch of salt

1 teaspoon vanilla

1 teaspoon flour

1 cup apricot jam

3 red grapefruit, peeled and sectioned with skin and pith removed

2 oranges, sectioned with skin and pith removed

3-inch round cutter

Preheat oven to 325°F. Whisk the flour, cornmeal and salt together in a small bowl. In a separate medium bowl using an electric mixer, cream the butter and sugar until smooth. Add 1 egg at a time until incorporated.

Using a rubber spatula, mix in the flour mixture until a dough is formed. Divide the dough in half and shape into discs. Wrap in plastic and chill for at least 30 minutes.

Remove one disc; roll between 2 pieces of wax paper to ⅛-inch thickness. Cut out 8 rounds. Place them on parchment-lined baking sheets 1-inch apart. Repeat with the remaining disc for a total of 16 rounds.

Pinch the edges of each round using thumb and forefinger to create a slight edge/lip. With a pastry brush, brush the rounds, including the edges, with egg wash. Bake until lightly browned, about 15 minutes, and set aside.

To prepare the pastry cream, combine the milk and half of the sugar in a small saucepan. Whisk briefly to combine and bring to a boil over medium heat, stirring occasionally. Meanwhile, in a separate, small bowl, whisk the yolks and salt together; then add the remaining sugar and vanilla, whisking until smooth. Sprinkle the flour over the surface and stir to combine.

Whisk ⅓ of the milk into the eggs to warm them. Then pour the warmed egg mixture into the saucepan and whisk constantly over medium heat. It will become thick quickly, so continue to whisk to prevent scorching or lumps from forming. Once the mixture comes to a boil, remove from heat and stir in vanilla. Cool. Press plastic wrap onto the surface to prevent a skin from forming and chill until ready to use.

To assemble, strain jam into a small saucepan and heat until warm. Brush each round with jam. Spoon a mounded tablespoon of pastry cream onto the center. With the back of the spoon, spread the cream over the surface until it reaches the raised edge. Arrange a few pieces of grapefruit and orange slices decoratively on top. Using a small pastry brush, carefully brush fruit and crust with jam.

All ingredients can be prepared up to 2 days in advance. Refrigerate cream and fruit and keep rounds in an airtight container. Canapés can be assembled up to 8 hours in advance.

———————— ⟲ ————————

Tips

No time to prepare the pastry? Good quality cornmeal biscuits, split in half, can serve as impromptu bases.

Twists

Pour rum over a mixture of raisins, dried cranberries, dried cherries, and small pieces of dried apricot and/or pineapple for 8 hours. Drain. Use in place of grapefruit and orange and omit the final glaze.

From left: Hazelnut Mousse Delights, page 48; Honey Cream Apricots, page 114.

Raspberry-Tangerine Bundles

This combination may seem pretty straightforward. Not when you taste it! Powerfully tart and sweet, inside each flaky pouch lies a perfect surprise.

Yield: 24 bundles

½ cup freshly-squeezed tangerine juice

2 tablespoons sugar

½ tablespoon tangerine zest

1 package phyllo dough, properly thawed

8 tablespoons (1 stick) unsalted butter, melted

2 cups raspberries

Combine the tangerine juice, sugar, and zest in a small saucepan. Over medium heat, stir as the mixture comes to a boil and continue to boil gently, stirring occasionally, until the mixture becomes thick and syrupy, about 10 minutes. Cool.

Lay phyllo out flat between 2 sheets of plastic wrap and lay a damp towel across the top. Remove 1 sheet, covering the rest again to prevent drying, and place it on a clean surface. Quickly brush the melted butter over the entire surface. Cut the sheet into squares measuring roughly 4 x 4-inches.

Preheat oven to 375°F. Stack 3 phyllo squares to form a star pattern (i.e., with the corners not lined up). Place 2 or 3 fresh raspberries in the center and drizzle 2 teaspoons of tangerine syrup over the berries. Lift the corners of the phyllo up and pinch together to create a small purse or bundle. Place on a parchment-lined baking sheet. Repeat, removing more phyllo sheets as needed, until you have 24 bundles. Brush bundles with more butter, and bake until golden brown, about 12 to 15 minutes.

Bundles can be prepared a week in advance. Arrange on a baking sheet, cover with plastic wrap, and freeze. No need to thaw before baking. Just pop them into the oven.

Tips

Leftover phyllo can be re-rolled in plastic wrap and refrozen for later use.

Twists

Leftover chopped dark chocolate, chopped nuts, and cake crumbs mixed together make a delicious last-minute filling, especially for chocolate lovers!

Lime Cream Squares

Mascarpone is an Italian "triple cream" cheese made by combining cream and whole milk. Along with accents of rum and lime, these little pillows are delicious as well as quick and easy to prepare.

Yield: 48 squares

1 egg yolk

2 tablespoons superfine sugar

1 cup mascarpone

2 tablespoons dark rum

Juice of ½ lime

2 sheets puff pastry measuring 9 x 12-inches (typically 1 package)

Egg wash (1 egg mixed with 2 tablespoon water)

8 kiwi fruit

48 small raspberries or blueberries, as garnish

In a small bowl, whisk together egg yolk, sugar, mascarpone, rum, and lime juice. Cover and chill.

Preheat oven to 375°F. Cut puff pastry into twenty-four 1½-inch squares each, for a total of 48 squares. With a pastry brush, brush each square with egg wash and place on parchment-lined baking sheets, 1-inch apart. Bake squares until puffed and lightly browned, about 15 minutes.. Cool.

Peel kiwi fruit and slice into ½-inch rounds. Cut each round into 6 wedges.

To assemble, spoon 1 tablespoon lime cream onto each square, then top with a fanned layer of kiwi slices. If pastry has puffed too high, don't hesitate to break the bubble: the lime cream will cover any 'scar' and you will have the level surface you need. Garnish with a raspberry or blueberry.

———— 6 ————

Tips

If you are uncomfortable using a raw egg, a cooked yolk will work fine.

Twists

Use clotted cream and fresh strawberries for a delicious tea-time sweet.

Caramelized Banana Canapés

Bananas are a fine fruit, mostly too familiar to be appreciated. Like fried plantains, however, bananas when sautéed take on an intensity seldom experienced. Served on sweet pastry with whipped cream, people will wonder, "why didn't I think of that?"

Yield: 40 canapés

1¼ cups flour

⅔ cup confectioners sugar

¼ teaspoon salt

8 tablespoons (1 stick) unsalted butter, frozen

1 large egg yolk

1 tablespoon heavy cream

½ teaspoon vanilla

3 tablespoons unsalted butter

1 cup dark brown sugar, firmly packed

4 large bananas, ripe but firm

½ cup chilled heavy cream, whipped

2½-inch round cutter

In a medium bowl, whisk together flour, confectioners sugar, and salt. Using the coarse side of a box grater, shred the frozen butter into the flour mixture. Quickly toss the butter pieces into the flour to get all of the butter pieces separated and covered with flour.

In a small bowl, combine egg yolk, heavy cream, and vanilla and pour into butter-flour mix. Using a pastry blender or your hands, gently mix the dough until it comes together. Pat into a disc, cover with plastic wrap, and refrigerate for 1 hour.

Preheat oven to 375°F. Roll dough to ¼-inch thickness and cut out 40 rounds. Pierce each round with a fork a few times and place on a parchment-lined baking sheet spaced 1-inch apart. Bake until brown around the edges and firm, about 15 minutes. Let cool.

In a medium frying pan on medium heat, melt the butter, add the brown sugar, and stir until it melts and combines with the butter. Slice bananas ¼-inch thick and sauté in the sugar-butter over medium heat until coated and just cooked through, about 2 minutes. Do not overcook: you want the bananas to keep their shape so they are easy to arrange.

To assemble, spread about a teaspoon of whipped cream on top of each pastry round. Place 3 banana slices on top of the cream and add a drizzle of the sugar sauce on top. Place completed canapés on a baking sheet under broiler just until the top gets crackly, about 1 minute.

Tips

Use up your overripe bananas, which are just fine when broiled. Just peel and freeze in a plastic bag first. This makes them easier to slice thinly.

Twists

Two cups of chopped strawberries sautéed in butter also work well. Just before taking them off the heat, add ¼-cup chopped, dark chocolate. Stir so the chocolate melts a bit and proceed as instructed.

Twelve Layer Bites

Testing this treat on my friends, everyone loved it, but no one could identify the flavor. Now that's commercial potential! The secret is a Cuban standard: guava jelly. Give your friends this crêpe-based quiz. The prize? Next time, winner makes all!

Yield: 32 boxes

4 cups sifted flour

4 large eggs

4 egg yolks

4 cups whole milk

3 tablespoons sugar

1 teaspoon salt

Butter for coating crêpe pan

16 ounces cream cheese

1⅔s cups guava jelly, divided

½ teaspoon lemon zest

3 tablespoons sweet white wine, divided

Fresh currants or small berries, as garnish

3-inch football shaped cutter or 1½-inch round cutter

Cupcake papers

Whisk flour, eggs, and yolks together in a medium bowl until smooth. Add milk, sugar, and salt and combine. Let the mixture rest for at least 30 minutes.

Heat a crêpe pan on medium-high heat and brush with a little melted butter to coat the pan. Pour ¼ cup crêpe batter into the pan. Swirl the mixture over the bottom of the pan until an even layer of batter coats the entire surface. Cook until one side is lightly browned, about 5 minutes. Turn crêpe over and cook for another minute. Slide crêpe onto a plate and repeat until you have 24 crêpes.

In a small bowl using a hand mixer, combine the cream cheese, 1 cup of the guava jelly, lemon zest, and 2 tablespoons wine together until smooth. Cover and chill until ready to use.

To assemble the crêpe stacks, place a heaping tablespoon of filling on a crêpe and spread it evenly over the entire surface. Top with another crêpe and repeat until you have a stack of 12 crêpes. Repeat with remaining crepes. Refrigerate the 2 stacks, covered, for 1 hour. Heat the remaining ⅔ cup guava jelly with 1 tablespoon of the white wine, stirring until smooth.

To assemble, remove 1 stack at a time and cut 12 shapes from each. Using a small pastry brush, liberally spread the warm guava on top. Place each shape onto a cupcake paper and chill to let the glaze set. Garnish with berries and serve at room temperature. Bites can be assembled up to 72 hours in advance.

Tips

When cutting shapes from each stack, start in the center first. The center tends to end up higher, and the pressure will push the filling outward, evening the thickness out.

Twists

Almost any jam, jelly, or filling can be used. Try watermelon pudding (page 92) for an unusual pairing.

Yin Yang Cakes, page 82.

Cake-Based Canapés

Are your dinner guests too demanding? Let them eat cake!

Dressed to impress, each of these unconventional confections is no small wonder. Several, like Saturn Petit Fours, use ganache with panache. Others offer new flavors (Watermelon Swirls) or dress old favorites in new clothes (Madeleine Peaches). Sensational inside and out, their good looks are just the icing on the cake.

- Strawberry Pineapple Dots
- Black Forest Cherry Boxes
- Madeleine Peaches
- Yin Yang Cakes
- Saturn Petit Fours
- Mini Cups of Cake
- Mini Watermelon Swirls

Strawberry Pineapple Dots

An impulsive stop into a Dutch Fair at a local church introduced me to my first homemade strawberry pineapple jam. Bought out of curiosity, each spoonful tasted better than the next, and pretty soon I'd eaten half the jar. I've never seen that homemade jam again, but the memory is forever in my taste buds. Couple that taste with bits of rich cake and you have a wonderful small version of pineapple upside-down cake.

Yield: 24 dots

¾ cup flour

2 tablespoons cornmeal

¾ teaspoon baking powder

¼ teaspoon salt

4 tablespoons unsalted butter, softened, plus extra for greasing pans

½ cup sugar

2 eggs, separated, room temperature

1 teaspoon vanilla

⅓ cup milk

1 tablespoon sugar

1 cup fresh pineapple, diced (drained, canned crushed pineapple can be substituted)

1 cup diced strawberries

4 tablespoons unsalted butter

¾ cup light brown sugar, firmly packed

24 cup miniature muffin pan (⅛ cup size cups)

Preheat oven to 350°F and grease muffin pans.

Combine flour, cornmeal, baking powder, and salt in a small bowl. In a medium bowl, cream the butter using an electric mixer for 30 seconds and add sugar. Beat at medium speed until the mixture is light and fluffy, about 2 minutes. Add egg yolks and vanilla and mix until combined. Add dry ingredients in 2 stages, adding milk in between and mixing each stage until combined.

In a medium bowl, beat egg whites on high speed until frothy; then add 1 tablespoon sugar and continue beating until egg whites are stiff. Fold egg whites into the dry mixture in 2 installments.

Mix the pineapple and strawberries together in a small bowl and reserve.

In a small saucepan, melt butter and brown sugar over low heat just until sugar is dissolved. While still warm, spoon a teaspoon into each muffin cup, top with 1 tablespoon of the fruit mix, then fill with batter up to the pan line. Do not overfill; you don't want the batter spilling over the edge as it expands.

Bake until golden brown, about 12 minutes. Remove pan from the oven and let rest for 1 to 2 minutes. While still warm, use a shallow kitchen tablespoon to loosen and remove each cake from the pan, being sure to scoop out the fruit at the bottom. Place on a plate, fruit-side up, to cool. You may need to adjust the fruit topping if it has shifted. Dots are best when served immediately; however, they can be covered with plastic wrap and kept in a cool place for up to 24 hours.

Tips

Soften the butter for the cake just until it can bend without cracking. Butter that is too soft results in a less-than-fluffy cake.

Twists

Replace strawberries with dried cranberries. Reconstitute with a little boiling water, cool, drain, chop, and sweeten.

Black Forest Cherry Boxes

One of my seminal cooking experiences came in high school when I got a job at a German bakery. The opportunity to see the inner workings of a bakery and to taste so many different German pastries was thrilling. I just "ate it up." That bakery is no longer with us (no, I was not their undoing), but I still remember the standard employee gift for every occasion: a black forest cake. It was a kind gesture, but I can't say anyone in my family relished the overpowering kirsch flavor.

These chocolate bites use sweet cherry wine, something a bit more tame than kirsch. My family just eats them up.

Yield: 35 boxes

1½ cups (3 sticks) unsalted butter, softened

2½ cups sugar

4 eggs

2 teaspoons vanilla

1 cup sour cream

1½ cups flour

½ cup cake flour

1 cup Dutch processed cocoa powder

2¼ teaspoons baking powder

½ teaspoon salt

3 cups fresh or frozen pitted cherries

½ cup sugar

¾ cup cherry juice

1½ cup sweet cherry wine

½ cup sweet cherry wine

1½ cup heavy cream, chilled

Mint leaves, as garnish

Grated chocolate, as garnish

Pastry bag fitted with ¾-inch star tip

Preheat oven to 325°F. Grease bottom and sides of a 9 x 11-inch baking pan. Using an electric mixer, beat butter in a large bowl until smooth. Add sugar and beat at high speed for 4 minutes; then at medium speed, beat in eggs one at a time. In a small bowl, mix vanilla into sour cream. In another medium bowl, sift the 2 flours, cocoa, baking powder, and salt. At low speed and in 3 stages, alternately add to the butter the dry ingredients and sour cream.

Spread batter evenly into prepared pan. Bake until cake springs back when touched, about 50 minutes. Cool.

Trim cake edges and cut cake into a 5 x 7 grid of thirty-five 1½ x 1½-inch squares.

To make the filling, combine cherries, and sugar in a medium saucepan. Cook over medium heat for 2 minutes. Add juice and 1½ cup wine and simmer until liquid is slightly reduced, about 5 minutes. Strain out cherries and return liquid to the saucepan. Boil until reduced to about ¾ cup, about 10 minutes. Pour over cherries and cool.

Carefully scoop out a well in the center of each chocolate box using a grapefruit knife. With a pastry brush, dab all surfaces with the remaining cherry wine.

In a small bowl, whip cream until thick and fluffy.

To assemble, gently spoon a little cherry filling into each carved well, mounding it a bit. Fill pastry bag with whipped cream and pipe a little burst on the side of each cherry mound. Garnish with a mint leaf and sprinkle with grated chocolate (see photo, page 85).

Tips

Freezing the cake before cutting will minimize crumbs and make it easier to cut evenly.

Twists

Cherries with cornbread in place of chocolate cake are an unconventional yet tasty combination.

Madeleine Peaches

Plenty of recipes look good but taste terrible. This was one of them. It took 20 years of determination and finally, the richness and firmness of Madeleine batter to turn this cookie exchange orphan into a prodigal success. What it carries inside is truly lovable.

Yield: 24 peaches

7 tablespoons unsalted butter

1 cup flour

½ tablespoon baking powder

6 tablespoons sugar

¼ teaspoon ground vanilla bean or
½ teaspoon vanilla extract

1 whole egg

1 egg yolk

2 tablespoons whole milk

2 teaspoons honey

1 tablespoon peach preserves, finely chopped

1 tablespoon cream cheese, softened

2 tablespoons almonds, finely chopped

Pinch of cinnamon

¼ cup fresh peaches, finely chopped

1 tablespoon peach brandy, optional

1 cup sugar

Red and yellow food coloring

2 tablespoons peach brandy

Whole cloves and small mint leaves, as garnish

Two 1½-inch half-round silicone molds (for 48 total)

Preheat oven to 350°F. Melt butter in a small saucepan. Sift flour and baking powder together in a medium bowl. In another medium bowl, using a whisk, combine sugar, vanilla, egg and yolk, milk, honey, and melted butter until incorporated. Fold into dry ingredients just until combined.

If using a non-silicone mold, brush with butter. Spoon a mounded measuring teaspoon of batter into each mold and bake until lightly browned, about 10 minutes. Don't worry, batter will melt down to fill the mold. Cool completely, then pop out of molds.

Using a sharp-tipped paring knife, cut a well out of the flat side of each round to hold the filling. Reserve the crumbs.

Combine ⅓ cup crumbs, peach preserves, cream cheese, almonds, cinnamon, fresh peaches, and brandy together in a small bowl until smooth.

Place sugar and 6 drops red food coloring in a container with a tight lid. Shake until sugar turns bright red. Pour half into another container and add 6 drops yellow food coloring; cover and shake until it is a light orange color.

To assemble, spoon a small amount of filling into each hollow and sandwich 2 filled half-rounds together to create a "peach." Fill and sandwich remaining half-rounds. With a small pastry brush, lightly brush/paint the outside of each peach with brandy. Roll each peach in the red sugar and then the orange sugar to coat. Attach 2 mint leaves with a clove for a stem.

Tips

In a rush, or don't have half-round molds? Use pound cake and a 1½-inch scoop to create the half-round cake shapes.

Twists

Add 1 teaspoon finely chopped lemon zest to the cake batter and replace filling with lemon curd (page 16). Roll sandwiched "lemons" in confectioners sugar, then yellow-tinted sugar.

Yin Yang Cakes

There are two symbols I've tried forever to render in a small dessert: the G clef and the yin yang. The one I've managed to figure out so far brings the duality of chocolate and vanilla into perfect harmony. And the G clef? Stay tuned!

Yield: 30-36 cakes

2 cups (4 sticks) unsalted butter, room temperature, divided

6 cups sugar, divided

14 eggs, room temperature, divided

4½ cups cake flour, sifted, divided

½ teaspoon salt, divided

2 cups heavy cream, divided

4 tablespoons vanilla, divided

1½ cups Dutch processed cocoa

1 cup heavy cream

1 tablespoon dry instant coffee

1½ pounds dark chocolate, coarsely chopped

1 cup heavy cream, whipped

2 pastry bags fitted with ¼-inch round tips

2½-inch round cutter

⅜-inch metal pastry tip

Line two 4 x 8-inch loaf pans with foil. Preheat oven to 350°F. Using a mixer with a paddle attachment, beat 1 cup butter and 3 cups sugar together for 5 minutes. Add 7 eggs, one at a time, beating to combine before adding the next.

In a medium bowl, combine 3 cups cake flour and ¼ teaspoon salt. Fold the flour mixture into the butter-sugar mixture in 3 stages, alternating with 1 cup of the cream in two ½-cup stages, beginning and ending with the flour. Stir in 2 tablespoons of vanilla.

Pour the batter into one pan and bake until the outside is golden brown and a cake tester inserted into the center comes out clean, about 60 minutes.

To prepare the chocolate cake, follow the same instructions. Simply substitute cocoa for half the flour.

To make the mocha ganache, heat cream and coffee to a boil in a saucepan and remove from heat. Pour over chocolate in a medium bowl and stir occasionally until smooth.

When cakes are cool, remove from pans and cut horizontally into three ¾-inch slices. Cut 5 to 6 rounds from each slice, 30-36 total.

Trace the pattern shown onto a clear plastic lid and carefully cut it out. Write "THIS SIDE UP" on one side of it. Using this template and a sharp paring knife, cut each round into opposing halves. Note that if you flip the template over at any point, you will have both "right" and "left-handed" yin yangs (see photo, page 74).

To assemble, using the tip of a small metal spatula, spread a layer of cooled ganache onto the inside curve of the vanilla shapes, then press the corresponding chocolate shapes onto them. Using the ⅜-inch pastry tip as a hole punch, punch out a small hole in the center of the yin and yang sections. Fill one pastry bag with mocha ganache and another with whipped cream. Fill the holes in the vanilla cakes with mocha ganache and the holes on the chocolate side with whipped cream.

Tips

Use a ruler to help you make uniform cake slices. Otherwise, widely varying widths will show up later when you fuse disparate halves together. Must have balance!

Twists

Add lemon flavoring and zest to one cake, pink food coloring to the other, and strawberry jam to join them. My friend calls these "Warholics Synonymous."

Clockwise: Stuffed Strawberries, page 26; Puddled Pears, page 20; Melon Flowers, page 14; Lemon Coconut Nests, page 16; Black Forest Cherry Boxes, page 78.

Saturn Petit Fours

I've always loved petit fours. To me, they are like delicate, edible flowers. At my German bakery job in high school, the last step before moving petit fours to the display case — namely, carefully using a pair of tweezers to place a silver dragee in the center of each sculpted rosebud — always happily fell to me.

But loving these delicacies was easier than making them at home. This celestial confection is a tribute to that time when everything tasted and looked "out of this world." To be honest, I don't think I've grown up yet!

Yield: 24 petit fours

1¼ cups sifted cake flour

¾ cup sugar, divided

1½ teaspoons baking powder

¼ teaspoon salt

3 large eggs, separated, room temperature

⅓ cup water

¼ cup vegetable oil

1 teaspoon vanilla extract

1 large egg white

¼ teaspoon cream of tartar

8 ounces dark chocolate, chopped

1 cup heavy cream

8 ounces white chocolate, chopped

¼ cup light corn syrup

Extra cocoa powder

1-inch melon baller

2-inch wide oval or round cutter

1-inch wide oval or round cutter

Small offset spatula

1 tablespoon fresh lemon juice

16 whole star anise, as garnish

Preheat oven to 325°F. Line a 9-inch loaf pan with foil and lightly spray with oil.

Sift flour, ½ cup of the sugar, baking powder, and salt in a medium bowl. Whisk together to blend and set aside. In a large bowl, whisk egg yolks, water, oil, and vanilla until blended. Stir in dry ingredients until combined.

In the bowl of an electric mixer using a whisk attachment, beat egg white and cream of tartar at medium speed until soft peaks form. Gradually beat in the remaining ¼ cup sugar; then increase the speed to high and beat until whites are stiff but not dry. Using a rubber spatula, fold egg whites into the flour-egg mix in 2 to 3 installments. Scrape batter into prepared loaf pan. Bake until cake is golden brown and a cake tester comes out clean, about 40 minutes. Cool completely, then freeze. Using a melon baller, carve out 24 balls and set aside.

Prepare the ganache coating by melting chocolate with cream in a small, heavy saucepan over med-low heat, stirring until smooth. Let stand until it has the thickness of thick cream, about 15 minutes. Line a baking sheet with plastic wrap and place a cooling rack across it. Spread cake balls out on rack and pour enough ganache over each to cover all sides. Do not turn balls or try to spread the ganache. It will run down the sides and cover the bottom. If you need more, scrape up what has collected in the pan and warm it back up in a double boiler. Let the finished cakes set until ganache is firm.

To make the rings, melt white chocolate over a small double boiler until smooth. Remove from heat and, using a wooden spoon, stir in corn syrup until it is completely incorporated. Line a baking sheet with plastic wrap and pour melted chocolate into the center. Fold plastic wrap over chocolate to cover completely and cool until pliable but not sticky, about 1 to 2 hours.

Using a heavy rolling pin, roll out white chocolate as thin as possible. Using the 2-inch cutter, cut out 24 shapes, then cut out 1-inch centers using the smaller cutter. Sprinkle cocoa powder over the rings.

To assemble, using a small offset spatula, transfer chocolate balls from rack to a serving plate. Carefully holding rings by their edges only, place one on each ball so that it fits snugly.

Tips

Freezing the cake before carving and coating results in easier carving and fewer crumbs.

Twists

Adding raspberry or almond paste centers is easy. Slice each frozen cake round in half and spread a little filling on one half. Press halves together and coat with ganache as described.

Mini Cups of Cake

Hostess with the mostest: this tribute to a old standard hides a chocolate ganache surprise.

Yield: 18 cupcakes

Yield: 18 cupcakes

8 ounces dark chocolate, chopped

1 cup heavy cream

2 ounces white chocolate, finely chopped

¼ cup heavy cream

5 tablespoons unsalted butter, softened

½ cup superfine sugar

¼ cup light brown sugar, firmly packed

1 egg yolk, room temperature, lightly beaten with a fork

1 teaspoon vanilla extract

1 cup flour

¾ teaspoon baking soda

¼ teaspoon salt

¼ cup buttermilk

2 large egg whites, room temperature

¼ teaspoon cream of tartar

¼ cup hot water

2 tablespoons light corn syrup

2½ cups confectioners sugar

¼ teaspoon vanilla

1 ounce unsweetened chocolate, chopped

¾ cup confectioners sugar

Whole milk

Miniature cupcake pan and papers (⅛ cup size)

Melt chocolate with cream in a small, heavy saucepan over med-low heat, stirring until smooth. Let stand until it has the thickness of thick cream, about 15 minutes. Roll into 18 balls measuring ¾-inch wide. Freeze.

Preheat oven to 350°F. Melt white chocolate over a double-boiler. In a separate saucepan, heat cream to boiling. Pour over chocolate and let stand for 1 minute, then stir until smooth. Set aside.

In a medium bowl, beat butter with an electric mixer for about 2 minutes until fluffy. Add superfine and brown sugars and cream until smooth. Add egg yolk and vanilla and mix to combine. Sift together flour, baking soda, and salt. Stir into butter mixture in 2 installments, alternating with buttermilk; then add white chocolate-cream and blend.

In a separate small bowl, using an electric mixer, beat egg whites and cream of tartar until glossy and firm but not forming stiff peaks. In 2 stages, fold egg whites into the batter until just combined.

Fill 18 muffin cups halfway, reserving remaining batter, and bake for 10 minutes. Remove pans and carefully press a frozen ganache truffle halfway into each cupcake. Distribute remaining batter evenly among cups and bake for another 5 minutes. Cool.

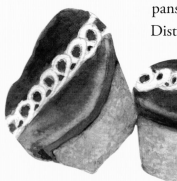

To prepare the icing, combine water and corn syrup in a small saucepan and bring to a boil. Remove from heat, stir in sugar until completely melted, then add vanilla.

Stir in chocolate until melted to a smooth and honey-like consistency.

Spoon onto cupcakes to form a puddle-like coating across the top. If icing begins to set, warm atop a double boiler until just warm and pourable.

In another small bowl, mix ¾ cup confectioners sugar with a few drops of whole milk until mixture is thick. Spoon into a small plastic bag, seal shut, and snip off a small tip off of one corner. Pipe a white squiggle on top of each cupcake.

Tips

To achieve a smooth, puddle effect with the icing, cupcake tops must be flat. Slice off any domed surfaces.

Twists

Bake cupcakes whole, cool, pipe lime curd into the centers (use lemon curd recipe on page 16 and substitute lime juice for lemon juice), dust with powdered sugar, and garnish with lime zest.

Mini Watermelon Swirls

There's something to be said for using what's in season. As much as I love watermelon, I hate to eat an underripe one, and it's the incomparable flavor of watermelon in its prime that makes this summertime sweet so special. The pick of the picnic for the gourmet set, the simple yet sophisticated pudding for filling never fails to amaze. Just remember, patience pays!

Yield: 28 swirls

1 pound ripe watermelon

2½ tablespoons sugar

2½ tablespoons cornstarch

Pinch of cinnamon

4 large eggs, room temperature

⅔ cup sugar

1 teaspoon vanilla

⅔ cup flour

¼ cup confectioners sugar

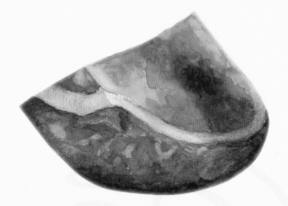

Cube watermelon and remove seeds. Put through a food mill or process in a blender to yield 1 cup of juice. Combine juice, sugar, and cornstarch in a medium saucepan. Bring to a boil over high heat, stirring constantly, until mixture thickens, becoming bright red. Stir in cinnamon. Pour into a glass dish to cool, placing a sheet of plastic wrap on the surface. Refrigerate until ready to use.

Preheat oven to 350°F. Line the bottom of two 8 x 12-inch baking pans with parchment paper. Grease and flour the paper.

In a medium bowl with an electric mixer, beat eggs and sugar on high until very thick and tripled in volume, about 6 minutes. Stir in vanilla.

Using a sieve and in 2 installments, sprinkle in flour and fold in gently with a rubber spatula until just blended. Spoon half the batter onto each pan and spread evenly. Bake until cake is golden brown, about 13 to 15 minutes. Cool until pans can be held barehanded. Place a sheet of parchment on the counter and sift confectioners sugar on top. Turn cake out onto parchment. Peel original parchment off. Roll cake up in the parchment in jelly-roll fashion and cool to room temperature. Repeat for second cake. Cakes can be rolled, covered with plastic wrap, and refrigerated, for up 24 hours. Cakes can also be frozen but be sure to thoroughly thaw before unrolling and filling.

To assemble, unroll cakes and spoon half the watermelon pudding onto each. Spread evenly up to ½-inch from the edge. Carefully re-roll cakes, using parchment paper as support and guide. Dust each roll with confectioners sugar and cut into ¾-inch slices.

Tips

When spreading the batter into each pan, spread to each edge evenly. The batter touching the pan edges "anchors" the batter in place while cooking.

Twists

Crème fraîche with small pieces of fresh or dried fruit makes an easy filling.

Tangerine Sharlotka, page 100.

Bread-Based Canapés

Unfortunately, man cannot live by bread pudding alone. Rich, buttery, bread-based desserts are — well, my "bread and butter." Because few things are easier or more comforting. Pamper yourself and satisfy your guests with the best thing since sliced bread.

- Cranberry Pear Bruschetta
- Toasted Banana Flowers
- Tangerine Sharlotka
- Ginger Honey Drops
- Polka-Dot Bread Pudding Squares

Cranberry Pear Bruschetta

I don't think Americans eat enough pears. Second to apples in the lunch box, pears don't score any better after dinner. But if students in my pie-making classes are any indication, this dessert just might change that. Just as cranberries are not confined to Thanksgiving, this colorful combination can be enjoyed year-round. Once you've tried it, I bet you'll be giving thanks a lot more often!

Yield: 12 bruschetta

6 slices firm white bread

8 tablespoons butter (1 stick), melted

2 firm pears

¼ teaspoon anise seed plus extra for garnish

1 cup fresh or dried cranberries

2 tablespoons water

¼ cup sugar

1 tablespoon cornstarch

2½ to 3-inch star cutter

Preheat oven 350°F. Carefully cut 2 stars from each slice of bread. With a pastry brush, coat both sides of each star liberally with melted butter. Place on a parchment-lined baking sheet and bake until the bread is golden brown and crisp, about 10 minutes.

Peel, core, and cut pears into about 8 pieces each. Crush anise seeds with a mortar and pestle to bring out the flavor. In a medium saucepan, bring pears, anise seed, cranberries, water, sugar, and cornstarch to a boil. Cook until cranberries are plumped and mixture is thick. Cool.

Spoon mixture onto stars and garnish with a few anise seeds. Serve at room temperature.

Tips

Topping stores well refrigerated for up to 5 days; bring to room temperature before assembling.

Twists

Use cherries, tart apples, and orange zest for a refreshing change. I guarantee your guests won't mind a bit.

Toasted Banana Flowers

Rich and sweet, caramelized bananas in tulip-shaped baskets. Simply elegant.

Yield: 24 flowers

24 slices firm white bread

2 sticks unsalted butter, melted

4 bananas

2 tablespoons unsalted butter

2 tablespoons light brown sugar

2 teaspoons almond extract

Almond slices or mint leaves, as garnish

2-inch round cutter

24 cup miniature muffin pan (⅛ cup size cups)

Cut 3 rounds from each bread slice to yield 72 rounds. Brush all rounds liberally with butter, front and back. Press 3 rounds into each cup, overlapping so they cover the bottom but don't protrude out the top.

Preheat oven to 350°F. Bake tulips until bread is crisp and golden brown, about 10 minutes. Cool completely.

Slice bananas ½-inch thick. In a medium frying pan, melt 2 tablespoons butter and sauté bananas until soft but not mushy, about 4 minutes. Add brown sugar and combine with a wooden spoon. Remove from heat and stir in almond extract.

Fill cups up to the point where the petals separate. Garnish with a mint leaf or sprinkle with almond slices (see photo, page 95).

———————— ☉ ————————

Tips

Be ready for surprise guests. Bake bread tulips and store in an airtight container for up to a month.

Twists

Fresh fruit, chopped nuts, and/or coconut flakes mixed and folded into whipped cream for filling make a quick and delightful way to use leftover ingredients.

Tangerine Sharlotka

Bread puddings of all kinds have always been a favorite and this mini jumbled Russian charlotte is most unique. Spiced pumpernickel and apples in a citrus cup? Even skeptics will find it surprisingly good.

Yield: 24 cups

12 small tangerines or clementines

2 tart apples, cored and chopped into ½-inch pieces

1 tablespoon lemon juice

8 tablespoons (1 stick) salted butter

¼ cup sugar

¼ cup tangerine juice

1 teaspoon cinnamon

½ teaspoon nutmeg

1 teaspoon vanilla

½ teaspoon salt

Zest of 2 tangerines

6 slices pumpernickel bread, crusts removed, torn into ½-inch pieces

Extra cinnamon, as garnish

Preheat oven to 350°F. Cut tangerines in half and using a grapefruit knife over a bowl, carve away most of the flesh, leaving about ¼-inch. Reserve juice. In a small bowl, toss apple with lemon juice to prevent browning.

In a medium saucepan, melt butter. Add apple, sugar, juice, cinnamon, nutmeg, vanilla, salt, and zest, and cook until the apple is softened and the liquid evaporates by ⅓, about 8 minutes. Add bread and sauté until bread is soft but not mushy, about 3 minutes. Cool the mixture for 5 to 10 minutes.

Spoon filling equally into tangerine cups (see photo, page 94). Place on a baking sheet and bake until bread crisps on top and juices start to bubble, about 30 minutes.

Sprinkle cinnamon on top. Can be served hot, cool, or at room temperature.

Tips

If filled tangerines are refrigerated overnight, the tang of the rind spreads into the bread, giving it added zing.

Twists

Use leftover rice pudding for filling. Sprinkle with cinnamon and bake until tops are browned.

Ginger Honey Drops

Here is gingerbread in the original sense of the word: a bread-based paste originating in the 14th century as a way to show off one's spices. Small loaves were made commercially much like these little bites, stamped with a decorative pattern and sold. You don't need to stamp these or charge your guests, but feel free to show off your dish's venerable provenance.

Yield: 24 drops

1 cup mild honey

¼ teaspoon, mounded, powdered ginger

⅛ teaspoon ground cloves

¼ teaspoon cinnamon

3 cups fresh whole wheat, rye, or pumpernickel bread crumbs (about 4 large slices of bread)

¾ cup walnuts, finely chopped

½ teaspoon ground ginger

Foil candy cups

Heat honey on medium heat in a medium-sized double boiler until it is hot but not boiling. Add ¼ teaspoon ginger, cloves, cinnamon, and bread crumbs. Cook until thick and sticky, about 15 minutes. Line a loaf pan loosely with plastic wrap. Scrape paste into pan and fold wrap over to cover. Cool.

In a small bowl, combine walnuts and ½ teaspoon ginger. Roll paste into 1-inch balls, then roll each in the nuts to coat and place in candy cup.

Tips

Don't undercook the paste or it will not set up firm enough to roll.

Twists

For a fancier presentation, sandwich paste between toasted walnut halves. These can be kept in a cool, airtight container for several days.

Polka-Dot Bread Pudding Squares

There are bread pudding lovers and there are chocolate lovers. It is my hope that this recipe will bring the two camps together. This rich but simple bread pudding is a speckled delight.

Yield: 16 squares

½ vanilla bean

1 cup heavy cream

1 cup whole milk

1 cinnamon stick (about 3 inches)

¼ pound brioche or rich white bread (about 3 large slices)

¼ pound chocolate bread or chocolate pudding cake

4 large egg yolks

½ cup sugar

½ cup chocolate chips

½ cup toasted hazelnuts, roughly chopped

8 tablespoons (1 stick) unsalted butter, melted

½ cup grated dark chocolate

Preheat oven to 325°F. Grease an 8-inch square baking pan and set aside.

Split vanilla bean in half; remove and reserve seeds. Place vanilla (pod and seeds), cream, milk, and cinnamon stick into a medium saucepan and bring to a boil. Remove from heat, cool for 30 minutes, then strain through a sieve.

Cut bread and cake into ½-inch squares. In a small bowl, whisk eggs and sugar. In a large bowl, combine milk-cream, egg-sugar, chocolate, nuts, and bread. Stir to combine.

When bread has absorbed all the liquid, transfer to prepared pan. Pack into pan evenly. Drizzle melted butter over the top and sprinkle with grated chocolate.

Bake until golden brown, about 45 minutes. Cool completely. Cut into 2-inch squares. Serve at room temperature or slightly warmed. Can be made several days in advance.

———————— 6 ————————

Tips

Leftover bread and cake can be saved up in the freezer until you have enough for this recipe.

Twists

Use dried fruit and nuts in addition to or in place of the chocolate.

Chocolate Malt Tulips, page 116.

Containers

Put the lid on a fantastic meal with a creative container dessert. Whether carved Lady Apple Crisp or molded Chocolate Malt Tulips, these show-stopping toppings in dramatic displays are sure to bowl them over.

- Stuffed Figs
- Peach Meringues
- Lady Apple Crisp
- Honey Cream Apricots
- Chocolate Malt Tulips
- Cinnamon Baked Florida

Stuffed Figs

Figs and brie are a match made in heaven. If you don't agree, rest assured that most of your guests will.

Yield: 8 figs

8 fresh figs

1 tablespoon honey

2 tablespoons butter, softened

½ cup pecans, finely chopped

½ teaspoon fresh thyme, minced

½ cup brie, rind removed, room temperature

Melon baller

Cut each fig in half vertically, keeping the stem in place. Using a melon baller, cut a well in each half.

In a small bowl, combine remaining ingredients into a paste. Fill wells and press fig halves back together. Serve as is or baked at 350°F until warm. Figs can be prepared up to 48 hours in advance and kept refrigerated until ready to serve.

Tips

If using dried figs, soften them in a bowl of boiling water for about 10 minutes.

Twists

Chop figs, combine all ingredients, and spread between 2 butter wafers (see page 50) for an unusually small dessert sandwich.

Peach Meringues

As a kid, I always liked the meringue part of my mom's lemon meringue pie best, especially the sugar tears that formed on top. These little bites bring back that memory — in a "peachy-keen" package.

Yield: 24 peaches

6 small peaches, unpeeled, quartered

¾ cup egg whites (about 6 eggs), room temperature

6 tablespoons sugar

1 tablespoon vanilla extract

3 tablespoons peach or apricot preserves

½ cup sliced almonds, plus extra for garnish

Preheat oven to 350°F. Pat peach quarters dry with paper towel and set aside.

In a small bowl, beat egg whites with an electric mixer at high speed until foamy. Add sugar gradually, continuing to beat whites until stiff. Add vanilla. Chop any large chunks of fruit in the preserves into small dice. With a rubber spatula, fold in preserves, then almonds.

Mound meringue into the well in each peach where the pit sat. Place onto a parchment-lined baking sheet and sprinkle with sliced almonds. Bake until meringues are golden brown, about 10 minutes. Cool slightly before serving.

Tips

The reddish part of the peach around the pit is typically bitter; it's best to trim it out.

Twists

For the sugar and almonds substitute light brown sugar and pecans.

Lady Apple Crisp

To me, apple crisp means Sunday dinner dessert at my grandmother's when I was a child. I still use her recipe, written in her handwriting on a faded index card. This little version of my favorite dessert results in a much crunchier topping than in the original, but the wonderful homey taste is still there. I hope it helps bring back a favorite memory for you.

Yield: 24 lady apples

24 lady apples or small round apples about 2-inches in diameter

¾ cup oats (not quick style)

¾ cup brown sugar, firmly packed

½ cup flour

8 tablespoons (1 stick) salted butter, cut into chunks

1 tablespoon vanilla extract

4 tablespoons butter

4 tablespoons brown sugar

4 cups peeled, coarsely chopped (½-to ¾-inch) firm apples (McCouns, Fuji, Gala)

Melon baller

Using a sharp knife, cut the top quarter off each apple and just enough off each base so that apples stand upright. Using a melon baller, scrape out the interior, leaving ¼-inch on the sides and ½-inch on the base (it is important to leave enough walls so the sides remains firm when steamed). Scraps can be used for applesauce.

In a steamer bring 1-inch water to a boil. Add apples, open side down, 4 or 5 at a time, and steam for no more than 1½ to 2 minutes. You want apples to soften a bit but not collapse. Cool.

Preheat oven to 350°F. To prepare the topping, place oats, brown sugar, and flour in a food processor and pulse several times to combine. Add butter chunks and process until butter is in pea-sized pieces. Add vanilla and pulse once more, making sure the mix remains rough and bumpy. Spread onto a parchment-lined baking sheet and bake, stirring occasionally until topping is lightly browned and resembles granola, about 15 to 18 minutes. Break up any large clusters and set aside to cool.

Melt remaining butter and sugar in a small frying pan. Add apples and sauté until slightly softened, about 6-8 minutes. They should still be a light golden color, not brown.

Mix ⅓ of the topping into the sautéed apples and fill hollowed apples to just below the rim. Sprinkle remaining topping on top (see photo, page 58) and serve at room temperature.

Filled apples can be covered and refrigerated for up to 2 days. Bring to room temperature and add topping before serving.

Tips

If lady apples are not available, check with your local farm. Most people don't want small apples, so they'll be glad you do.

Twists

For a raw, healthy version, brush carved apples with lemon juice to prevent browning. Mix chopped apple with thick yogurt, almonds or sunflower seeds, and honey.

Honey Cream Apricots

Cardamom has a unique, practically indescribable flavor. It can easily be found in the spice section of any grocery, yet in this country it's not often used. Once tasted, however, I bet you'll be hooked as much as I've been from the start.

Yield: 24 apricots

12 small fresh apricots

½ cup heavy cream, chilled

1 teaspoon cardamom, ground

¼ teaspoon vanilla

¼ cup honey

Thyme sprigs, as garnish

Cut each apricot in half horizontally and remove pits.

In a small bowl, beat cream to stiff peaks. Fold in cardamom and vanilla. Fill apricots, mounding the cream, in the center. Drizzle honey over the top and garnish with a thyme sprig.

Tips

If fresh apricots are not available, soft, plump, dried apricots also work. Do not cut in half; cut a slit into the side to fill (see photo, page 65).

Twists

White raisins have a slight apricot flavor. Simply fold raisins into filling and serve in a fancy wine glass.

Chocolate Malt Tulips

I'm haunted by moth balls. That's what my sister and I used to call malt balls as children. My last visitation came when I tasted a vanilla malted cookie. I was flooded with memories of how much my mother loved vanilla ice cream malteds. Of course I could not rest until I found a way to incorporate that childhood flavor into a small dessert. This is it: a "plain old" chocolate malt in a fancy new package.

Yield: 20 tulips

⅓ cup light corn syrup

8 ounces semi-sweet chocolate, chopped

1 cup heavy cream, chilled

½ teaspoon sugar

4 tablespoons malted milk powder

Cocoa powder, as garnish

3-inch football shaped cutter

Pastry bag fitted with a star tip

Melt chocolate over a small double boiler until smooth. Remove from heat and using a wooden spoon, stir in corn syrup until completely incorporated. Loosely line a baking sheet with plastic wrap. Add chocolate and fold wrap over to cover completely. Cool until pliable but not sticky, about 1 to 2 hours. Molding chocolate can be stored double-wrapped in an airtight container for about a week.

Roll chocolate between 2 layers of plastic wrap as thin as possible; ideally about ⅛ inch. Cut out 60 leaves. Press sets of 3 leaves together at the base to create 20 "tulips" (see photo, page 106). Place them uncovered on a parchment-lined baking sheet to firm up, about 30 minutes.

Whip cream and sugar together in a medium bowl to stiff peaks and fold in malt powder. Fill the pastry bag with malted cream and pipe into flower centers, then sprinkle with cocoa powder.

⟨᎐⟩

Tips

Any petal shape will create an attractive flower, so use whatever cutter shape you have available.

Twists

Use fresh berries for filling on whipped cream or your favorite mousse.

Cinnamon Baked Florida

Head south for the winter; or rather, to the Middle East. This exotic flavor combination can be enjoyed even in January, the height of citrus season.

Yield: 8 oranges

4 small oranges

2 teaspoons cinnamon

2 egg whites (¼ cup), room temperature

¼ teaspoon cream of tartar

3 tablespoons superfine sugar

¼ cup orange marmalade

Cinnamon or zest of 1 orange, as garnish

Preheat oven to 350°F. Cut each orange in half horizontally. Slice just enough off the bottom of each half so that halves sit upright. Using a grapefruit knife, cut out flesh and reserve in a small bowl. Carefully pull remaining membrane away so a clean cup remains.

Drain orange pieces, sprinkle in cinnamon, and toss gently. Spoon equally into cups. Filled cups can be covered with plastic wrap and refrigerated for up to 2 days.

To make the meringue, in a small bowl using an electric mixer, beat egg whites and cream of tartar together until they are frothy; then very slowly add sugar until egg whites are thick, white, and hold a stiff peak when beaters are removed. Carefully fold in marmalade until combined.

Spoon meringue atop each filled cup. Place on a baking sheet and bake until the meringue is browned, about 5 to 8 minutes. Sprinkle cinnamon or orange zest on top. Meringue cups can be prepared up to 1 hour in advance.

Tips

Before filling cups, use a paring knife to cut a decorative edge.

Twists

Combine orange pieces with cranberries and walnuts or pomegranate seeds and hazelnuts, and garnish with brown sugar.

Tropical Berry Kabobs, page 24.

Resources

Atlantic Spice Company
North Truro, MA
800-316-7965
www.atlanticspice.com
Wide assortment of cooking spices.

The Baker's Catalog
Norwich, VT
800-827-6836
www.kingarthurflour.com
Specialty foods, chocolate, cookie cutters, and more.

Bergen Supply Company
Pearl River, NY
845-735-4674
www.cookking.com
Professional-grade cooking utensils and equipment.

The Chef's Warehouse
Bronx, NY
718-842-8700
www.ChefsWarehouse.com
Source for high-end pastry ingredients and equipment.

House on the Hill
Elmhurst, IL
877-279-4455
www.houseonthehill.net
Assorted cookie cutters.

J.B. Prince
New York, NY
800-473-0577
www.jbprince.com
Professional grade bakeware and equipment.

La Cuisine
Alexandria, VA
800-521-1176
www.lacuisineus.com
General equipment for cooking and baking and a wide assortment of cookie cutters.

LorAnn Oils
517-882-0215
www.lorannoils.com
Gourmet flavorings, vanilla, food coloring, and candy making equipment and supplies.

New York Cake and Baking Distributors
New York, NY
800-94-CAKE-9
www.nycake.com
General bakeware and cookie cutters.

Penzey's Spices
Muskego, WI
800-741-7787
www.penzeys.com
Great source for spices and herbs.

Scandicrafts Cuisine Internationale
Camarillo, CA
800-966-5489
www.scandicrafts.com
Silicone molds, bakeware, and baking utensils.

Sur la Table
Seattle, WA
800-243-0852
www.surlatable.com
Decorative baking equipment, cookie cutters, utensils, and more.

Sweet Celebrations
Edina, MN
800-328-6722
www.sweetc.com
Baking equipment, pastry tips, cookie cutters, decorative sugars, dragees, and more.

Williams-Sonoma
San Francisco, CA
877-812-6235
www.williams-sonoma.com
Baking equipment, specialty foods, cookie cutters, and more.

Wilton Industries
Woodridge, IL
800-994-5866
www.wilton.com
Cookie cutters, pastry bags, tips, and assorted bakeware.

In my life I've found that when it comes to donating time or energy to a cause, it is important to be doing something one enjoys. I know I keep commitments longer when I'm surrounded by people and/or things that I love, so it is probably not surprising that most of my charity work has had something to do with food. I can be planning a Victorian Tea fundraiser or washing off cans at a local food pantry; it doesn't matter. Working on the *Tastefully Small* series, I realized that it too gives me another opportunity to share not just what I love but through what I love.

Know that a portion of the proceeds from this series will be given to America's Second Harvest Network, an umbrella organization supporting over 50,000 food charities in the U.S. For more information, visit **www.secondharvest.org**.

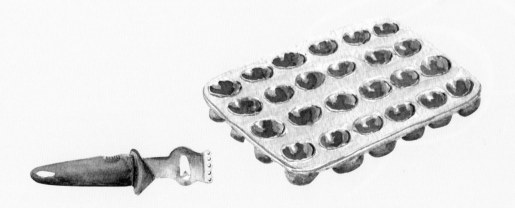

Choco-Ginger Sandwiches, page 54.

Index